Elizabeth M. Potter /
Beatrix Potter (contributor)

Beatrix Potter
Painting Book part 9

by
Elizabeth M. Potter

Content   Page

Colouring pictures

I.   The story of Peter Rabbit and Father Christmas   3
II.   The story of Peter Rabbit and the fairies   11
III.   The story of Peter Rabbit and the tea party   19
IV.   The story of Peter Rabbit and Jimmy Chipmunk   27
V.   Original book illustrations   35
VI.   Further books of Elizabeth M. Potter   40

Bibliografische Information der Deutschen Nationalbibliothek:
Die Deutsche Nationalbibliothek verzeichnet diese Publikation in der Deutschen
Nationalbibliografie; detaillierte bibliografische
Daten sind im Internet über http://dnb.dnb.de abrufbar.

© 2018 Elizabeth M. Potter 1. Auflage
Covergrafik, Texte und Bilder: © 2018 Elizabeth M. Potter

Herstellung und Verlag: BoD – Books on Demand, Norderstedt

ISBN: 9783752866520

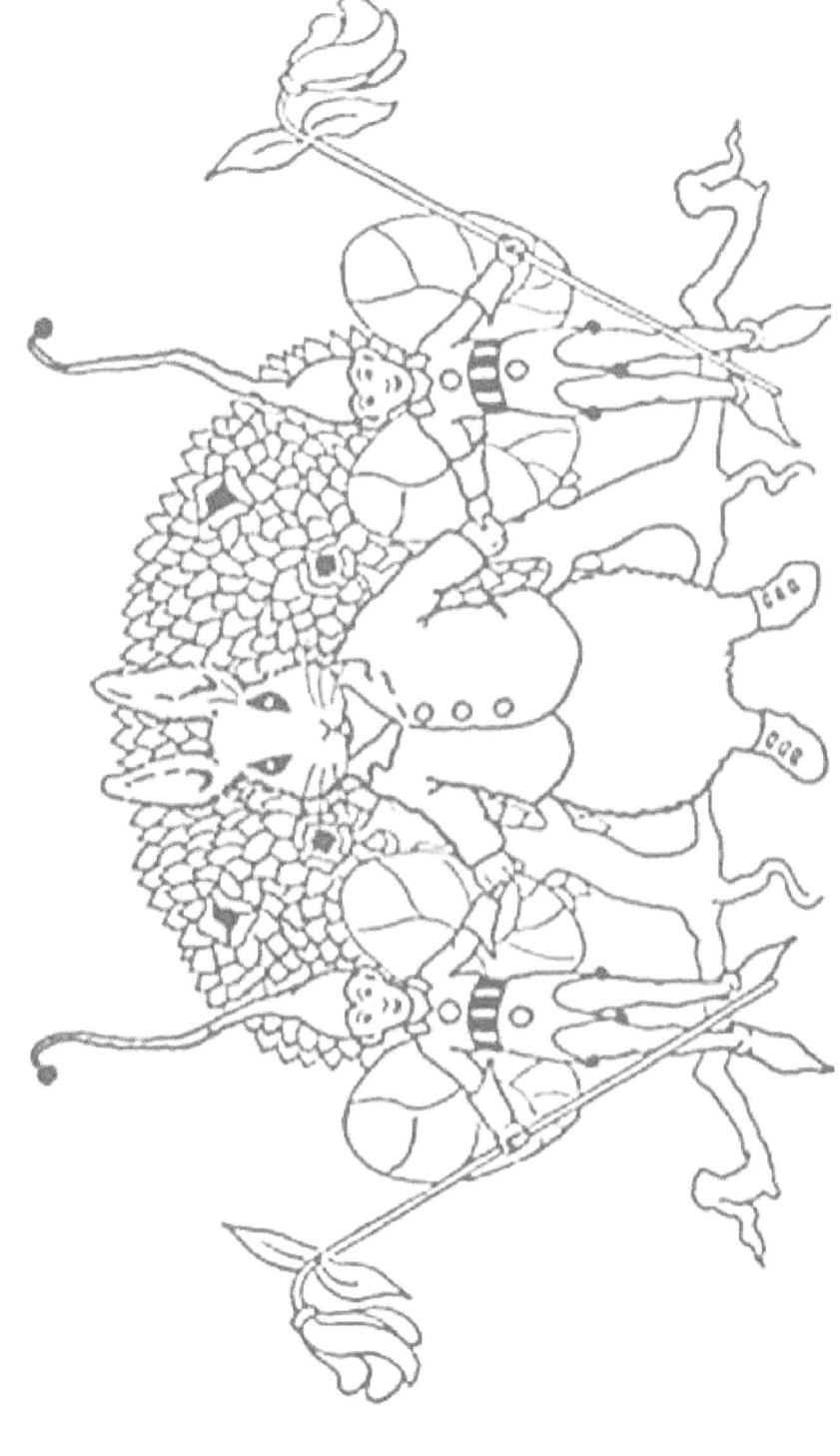

Further books of Elizabeth M. Potter

NOTEBOOKS
The Peter Rabbit Notebook
PAINTING BOOKS
Beatrix Potter Painting Book Part 1 (Peter Rabbit)
Beatrix Potter Painting Book Part 2 (Peter Rabbit)
Beatrix Potter Painting Book Part 3 (Peter Rabbit)
Beatrix Potter Painting Book Part 4 (Peter Rabbit)
Beatrix Potter Painting Book Part 5 (Peter Rabbit)
Beatrix Potter Painting Book Part 6 (Peter Rabbit)
Beatrix Potter Painting Book Part 7 (Peter Rabbit)
Beatrix Potter Painting Book Part 8 (Peter Rabbit)
Beatrix Potter Painting Book Part 9 (Peter Rabbit)
Beatrix Potter Painting Book Part 10 (Peter Rabbit)
Peter Rabbit Painting Book
CLIPART BOOKS
Beatrix Potter 99 Cliparts Book Part 1 (Peter Rabbit)
Beatrix Potter 99 Cliparts Book Part 2 (Peter Rabbit)
Beatrix Potter 99 Cliparts Book Part 3 (Peter Rabbit)
Beatrix Potter 99 Cliparts Book Part 4 (Peter Rabbit)
PASSWORD BOOKS
The Peter Rabbit Passw ortbook